A HARVEST OF OUR DREAMS

with
ELEGY FOR THE REVOLUTION

Poems by
KOFI ANYIDOHO

LONDON
HEINEMANN
IBADAN   NAIROBI

Heinemann Educational Books Ltd
22 Bedford Square, London WC1B 3HH
PMB 5205, Ibadan · PO Box 45314, Nairobi

EDINBURGH   MELBOURNE   AUCKLAND
HONG KONG   SINGAPORE   KUALA LUMPUR
NEW DELHI   KINGSTON   PORT OF SPAIN

Heinemann Educational Books Inc.
70 Court Street, Portsmouth, New Hampshire 03801, USA

British Library Cataloguing in Publication Data

Anyidoho, Kofi
  A harvest of our dreams.—(African writers series; 261)
  I. Title   II. Series
  821   PR9379.9.A/

ISBN 0–435–90261–X

Set in 10/12 pt Palatino by
Wilmaset, Birkenhead, Merseyside
Printed in Great Britain by
Richard Clay (The Chaucer Press) Ltd, Bungay, Suffolk

Contents

∿∿∿∿∿∿∿∿∿∿∿∿∿∿∿∿∿∿∿∿∿∿∿∿∿∿∿∿∿∿∿∿∿∿
∿∿∿∿∿∿∿∿∿∿∿∿∿∿∿∿∿∿∿∿∿∿∿∿∿∿∿∿∿∿∿∿∿∿

For all the Students of Ghana
   Who risked their flesh to
   Clip the Panther's Claws . . .

   A Luta Continua!!!

   *   *   *

And for my Sisters:
   Afua, Aku, Exi kple Xetsa
   And of course for Enyruie Kodzovi Anyidoho
   And for Papa Kpodo Yotuvo
   In memory of Dada Adidi Abla Anyidoho:

   She went too soon to see our Harvest Dance.
   But she sang for us she left for us
   The haunting gift of Song.

   *   *   *

And for Akosua my Wife
   And Akua and Akofa our Children
   And their children's children's Child.

PART ONE

SEEDTIME

Mythmaker

for George Dakpo, S. O. Smith, Adjei Barima:
they lost their lives in student risings against the Panther's boast.

The children are away
The children are away
The children
These children are away
away in schoolrooms where the world in book
distils daydreams into visions
burns memorials of the past
in bonfires of the soul

What shall we say to Mythmaker
when and if he comes?

Nothing.

He will come and find for himself
how our history gathered discarded myths
from peddlers of rumours and bearers of tales
and with a few conjunctions of the law
constructed a new constitution
for the union of our several selves

The children
These children are
away miles away from home
plucking poison kisses from laurels
blooming with rage in mid-winter.
Some day they will be home.
They will turn and return
with garlands for their land
But they will sigh to see how for six seasons

our mothers fed on new dirges
our common *kenkey* grown so lean
we needed a decree to insure her health
our scholars, deployed from campuses
into ghost communal farms,
walked the streets at dawn like zombies
peddling posters proclaiming final obsequies
for the revolution that went astray.
They will be hit by stray bullets
They will be clubbed to death in dark corners
And we will hear of brassband processions
congregating at our Castle of despair
celebrating the victory of our death . . .

The children are away
The children are away
The children
These children are
away.
Some day they will be home
for final rites for the late renegades.
Their garlands will pass for wreaths.
And yet somehow they won't be sad or mad.
They will turn and return to a bereaved home
and still they won't be mad or sad.
Though our memory of life now boils
into vapours, the old melody of hope
still clings to tenderness of hearts
locked in caves of stubborn minds.

The children will be home
The children will be home
The children
Those children will
                   be home
                   Some Day.

Maamobi, Accra, 1 June 1977

Seedtime

Do not search too hard
for words to trap these thoughts
the thoughts that bring the tears
upon the harvest of our dreams.

They say our thoughts are threads, crossing
and criss-crossing into new cobwebs of life
And
I shall spin a handful of hopes
against this cutback in our dreams
against this wild backlash of screams
even against these lingering doubts
at testing time for our faith in Gods

We load our voice with these burdens
searching myths for miracle drugs
distant cures for our sickness of the soul

This land survived the flood of birthwaters
but moonmen came with gifts of thunder
so we drank a barrel of moonshine
and lost seedtime in seasons of harvest dance.

But Sungod comes to claim his own at harvest time.
At heaven's other gate a friendly soul appears
wearing a gown of velvet flames:

There is no curse on us
he sings
There is no curse on us

We who bought fevers from pawnshops of the world
And tread byways with burdens in our voice

There is no curse on us
There is no curse on us

Our orphan laid an egg across the backyard of the skies
The rainstorm came and swept it all away
Again he laid an egg across the backyard of the skies
Again the rainstorm came and swept it all away
Today he sows a mystery seed in the bosom of whirlthoughts
Our predator birds shall have to prey upon
their own anger their own nightmares

We will not die the death of dreams
We will not die the cruel death of dreams

There will be anthems sung for victories reaped in dreams

Our harvest-gatherers crawl on granary floors
poking naked fingers into armpits of the soul
and laughter comes rolling through our voice of tears
weaving the season's final dance for miracle-makers
and now we must wear this gown of flames
and walk on stilts across mirages
in these deserts of our soul
And mythmaker shall draw the shrouds apart
And there in the wake of screams
we embrace a voice wearing our dreams

And so we find the voice to trap these thoughts
These jogging hopes for a harvest of our dreams

There is no curse on us
There is no curse on us

We will not die the death of dreams
We will not die the cruel death of dreams.

Bloomington, Indiana, 1–12 April 1979

A Harvest of Our Dreams

There is a ghost
on guard
at Memory's door

scaring away these pampered hopes
these spoiled children of our festive days

The honey bee had plans in store
for his Mother-Queen: he went across the world
gathering fragrance from dreamy waterlilies
from lonely desert blooms
Some other gatherer came with plans
all for his own desires
Our hive went up in flames. I was away.

We will hum a dirge for a burden of these winds

Memories of our honeycomb floating through
seedtime within the soul beyond the reach of Song
Rowdy echoes burst upon our soul's siesta

And harvests go ungathered in our time

There will be strange voices filling spaces
in our mind, weaving murmurings upon
the broken tails of songs abandoned once in playing fields
Rumblings from our past are planting stakes
across our new rainbows
and in seasons of harvest dance
there still will be a ghost
on guard
at Memory's door

6

It was for shame the turtle
hid his pain beneath his shell
and crawled upon the pleasures of the sea.
His secret pain became a hidden rottenness
a poison to his smiles

We will hum a dirge for a burden of these winds

Memories of our honeycomb floating through
seedtime within the soul beyond the reach of Song
Rowdy echoes burst upon our soul's siesta

And harvests go ungathered in our time

So these echoes come in ritual dance
from old homesteads where once she often sang
singing the dirge keeping the wake at endless funerals

Ootsa of the sea. I am Ootsa of the sea.
I did not know it would be like this for me:
Yevu's net has caught me with my dreams.

And now we tread byways
searching passing faces
for fleeting image after image
seeking kindred minds
for lost passwords into fiestas of the soul

Somehow we know the carnival days
cannot be gone so soon
We may gather again those
unfinished harvests of our soul.
Uncle Demanya shall come back home
with the bread basket of which
he sang through life across the hunger of our graves

Uncle Demanya shall come back home
with the bread basket of which
he sang through life across the hunger of our graves.

Bloomington, 4 February–1 April 1979

The Hyena's Hymn

for Obiba

They will come this way some day
these demigods with broken oaths
for a harvest of our dreams
They will come seeking lonely paths
through our famished dreams
to the house of exiled gods

I will make music with howls of dogs
I will borrow the shrieks of witches
the screeches of dancing monkeys
I will make music with howls of dogs

When the Christ strayed into
our village one shroudy Easter dawn
our people took him for a ghost
It was not their fault: He was
standing upon the grave of a destooled chief
the chief who stole the diviner's oracle bag
and stole his children's bowl of soup
and pawned his oaths for a brief season of grace.
He had a monster child who died before the outdooring.

So when the pastor came dancing in
pursued by disciples selling hosayanas
Our people stood before the cemetery gates
reminding the gods to protect their children's
souls against these messengers of death.

I went into our parliament home
seeking audience with Speaker's chair.
They said I must have just returned from farm:
Parliament had gone on sudden leave
prior to retirement.
They misdirected me to our Castle
where they gave me forms to fill
still standing at the gates.
I said I had a dream
to place before the military governor's
Boots –
I am a visionary, you know?
only so far my visions have been
of things we didn't do things we could have done –
They said our Castlemen were all dizzy
making grand visions from dreams of fallen gods
and in any case I was not properly dressed
and my name could not be found
in the register of co-opted councilmen
I pulled out my birthplace card
They said it had no official signature
I swear ma papa and ma mama born me
long long before they born them 'lectoral commissioner
They laughed. Yes, those sons of thugs and whores
They laughed and asked if
I wanted a noonday bowl of flames
They said I could give my dreams
to our birthplace dogs or
just dump them on the dunghill.

In absence of a Chief Justice
I file my appeal at the low court of Memory.

because I am ignored because
because I am abandoned to my dreams
I lay ambush within my soul
preying upon prenatal doubts
nostalgias of my broken world
and if
they should come this way some day
those demidogs with broken oaths
for a harvest of our dreams
if by some curse they should
come seeking those lonely paths through our famished dreams

I will make music with howls of dogs
embrace their groans with laughter from our wounds
flood their graves with hurricanes of our blottled joys.
I will borrow the shrieks of witches
the screeches of dancing monkeys

I will make music with howls of dogs.

Legon, 8 September 1977

The Diviner's Curse

again for Obiba

Your prayers my people
are doing a dance of ghosts
upon the courtyard of my song
and I wake to meet
my voice running naked
across our house of storms

    a diviner foretells a groan
    beneath the joy of birthday feasts
    a drunken brother drags the oracle bag
    into a harvest bonfire
    cowries scream above the roar of brushfires

I too wonder at the zeal of these prophets who
come offering half-truths for a harvest of our dreams
I marvel at the glory in their vision
the smile around the corners of their voice

I know some day they will be home
The children will come pointing questions at
Us.
Do we not welcome these prophets here
with communal ritual feasts
see them go with lips besmeared with he-goat fat?

The children will come pointing questions at
Us.
Here I stand mumbling apologies into my beard
I spend a fortune rehearsing
the lies we shall have to tell
to explain our manhood's failure in prime of youth.

I teach myself to be wily as the tongue
to move with craft among the knife-throwers

Thus I become a coward
to the courage of our thoughts

And the children shall come pointing questions at
Me.

Hohoe, 21 December 1977

~~~~~~

PART TWO

AKOFA
~~~~~~

woman! woman!
how often you carry the heaviness
of your soul . . . only to empty it into songs . . .

Atukwei Okai, 'Lorgorligi Logarithms'.

Blewuu

Blewuu . . . blewuu . . . , Akofa, blewuuu . . .
Words are birds: They fly so fast too far
for the hunter's aim. Words are winds:
Sometimes they breeze gentle upon the smiles
our hearts may wear for joy. They fan the sweat
away from fever's brow. They lull our minds
to sleep upon the soft breast of Earth.
Yet soon too soon words become the mad dreams
of storms: They howl through caves through joys
into shrines of thunderbolts. They leave a ghost
on guard at memory's door. Therefore
gently . . . gen-tly . . . Akofa, ge-nt-ly . . .
take care what images of life
your tongue may carve for show
at carnivals of weary souls

Nunya

Ha . . . ha . . . ha . . . ha . . . ooo . . . yi!
Let me laugh a small laugh as though
my heart were doing a little dance of joy.
Your tongue, our brother, is a dawn breeze
spreading peace upon an orphan's fear for eyes
of day but my mother's husband's youngest son
do not eat salt and give yourself heartburns.
I know you've seen the world through windows
in your school, and they say your view is sharp.
Yet you are only our little darling master.
I saw my moon in many many skies before
your sun first raised his head into our clouds.
Please please do not frown and sneer into my face.
I do not deny that even a child may have wisdom.

But the wisdom of the child is a piece of broken pot
in the sand. The toddler may claim it for his own
hold it to his bosom and fight a duel to keep it still.
Yet for all his mad pleasure
it is only a broken piece.
This child owner of great treasure
what can he tell of what became
of the other broken pieces? How
could he tell the shape of the pot
that broke and lost the dreams it cooked
for how many feasts for how many Moons?
And who could the porter be?
The head that first carried the image
of that pot the hands which gave that image
to the world what may have become of them?

So you see my mother's master child?
There is no absolute knowledge
to the waywardness of life's byways.
These little cassava sticks of mine
have left their mark on several tracks of life.
But the thing I chased exchanged his feet for wings
and I am a hunter come home with a basketful
of wild tales of how it is today that the cooking pot
must sleep mouth-down in a corner of the old kitchen.

Dàdá

I remember how mother sat me down upon her thighs
and drank the joy from my eyes
her lips poised uncertain upon
the brim of a smile that never
once blossomed into wild petals of joy.
With the child's abundant faith in life
and a crowded world I screamed

with mirth to teach her smile to bloom.
But now with all these cracks in faith,
behind mother's smile of joy of love
I see those stumps of joys cut down in mid-season.
The pot in which she cooked her dreams
fell and broke in the sand and she was searching
for lost childhoods on shores of my beauty's dawn.

Tugbedzevi

I remember well the coming of that dawn.
How I woke up from the naughty sleep
of the carefree child and found
a gentle dream coiling on my bed
her head upon my bosom for a pillow.
I tied her well around my ripening waist
to hold my little passion cloth.
And when I stepped outside into the world beyond our house
I caught my beauty's dawn peeping over our fence
hiding behind the trees behind our house behind
the things that hide behind those shadows in our mind.
Still drowsy from my sleep I yawned
and stretched myself into a bow and
arrows from my breast shot into the dawn
and caught beauty weaving a pubertal dance
in ritual feast of dream and dawn and hope.

And I remember well yes I remember
But how can I forget all those early
morning joys grumbling through the dew
to wake the river with our chattering
whispering teasing gossips about
the foolishness of boys who thought
their voice was grown quite big enough
to bear the weight of burdens they could give.

Sometimes we talked of funny old men with
the waist of the wasp. They kept asking
useless questions sending boring greetings
to your parents casting sly glances
at things too fresh for their souring tastes.

Tsitsa

And then of course we argued about teachers
those teachers in the school. We all agreed
they really could be funny. I mean sometimes.
There was the big man Masita Matiasi himself.
They say he went to koledzi somewhere up
in the mountains of Amedzofe. Then he went again
to another koledzi also up and up in the chain
mountains of old Akropong or was it Abetifi?
Now I cannot even tell. Anyway, it was always
on mountains. So when he came down
to this village in the valley his head was full of skies.
He talked about Mawu Yehowa without swallowing saliva.
May be Mawu was his Grand Father.
As for Inglishi, he could speak it better than an Ako.
Sometimes his pupils licked those big big words
rolling down his tongue into his he-goat beard.
Sometimes too those rolling words fell down on his belly.
He had the belly of a toad and he always
talked pulling up his ancient trozasi.

Awoyo

Awoyo crossed my path and spat upon my toes.
I did not cough.
She went away strutting about
and stepped upon a thorn.
She came right back and spat into my face.

I did not even sneeze.
She shuffled away with a scowl on her evil face
hoping she was smiling.

I sit down here thinking she'll bring herself again.
I will slash her with my tongue
and spread hot pepper in her wounds.
The witch daughter with the face of an owl.
Awoyo, come back here and
I will sing to you your shame.
That night you went talking to
every stick and every little rope
swearing you caught Agbenoxevi on top of me
doing some funny thing behind your smelly mother's
broken fence. You must have walked out
straight from a strange nightmare.

Come Awoyo come back here and
I will give it back to you give to you
the thing Agbenoxevi told you once
at a gathering of the youth. He said
he would not take a hundred Awoyos.
Not even for a gift. He said even
if your mother gives you a ritual bath on Christmas Day
if she covers up your nakedness in velvet robes even
if she hangs diamond pearls about your stringy neck
and gives you away with a live turkey and eggs and all
He Agbenoxevi would send you back at noon
to wherever you may have found your strange beauty.

Today for me is like your yesterday.
You're glad he's gone away from me.
But he will be back. I know he will be back.
Though now you cross my path and spit into my face.
You spread rumours I have no womb for birth that
at my age I must begin to think of grandchildren.

Awoyo I am not the whore's daughter like you
Your mother went from this village to that village
shitting babies all along her path across the clan.
Did she ever suggest to you
who your papa could have been?
They say the day she died the elders sighed
and poured a long libation on her grave
praying her soul to come next time somewhat reformed.

You witch daughter with the face of an owl
Come cross my path again
I will spread your shame for you to crawl upon.

Fertility Game

In a public performance the opening line should be repeated by the
audience throughout the entire poem.

Come back home Agbenoxevi come back home

A week today at carnival time
youngmen of the land will gather
for the wrestling duel of song and dance,
maidens will sharpen their tongues and
carve praise images of dream lovers and
I have a gourdful of praise names laid aside for you

Come back home Agbenoxevi come back home

In the eyes of town
I will break the evil glance of witches
I will pour you a calabash of pride
I will hold it firm to your lips
till your eyes catch the glimpse of stars
till your mind reaches out for moons
till your body vibrates to rhythms of the seas

Come back home Agbenoxevi come back home

and your voice shall rise deep across the years
through rainbow gates to the beginnings of things
It will come floating through seasons of glory
thundering through deserts and painfields where
our people died the death of droughts and of wars
where they died and lived again
where they die and wake up
with seeds of life sprouting from their graves

Come back home Agbenoxevi come back home

Agbenoxevi Atsu Agbenoxevi
I have held my passion in check for you
holding it fast against storms against thunder
held it firm against the haunting smiles of gods.
I have strained my bosom against the sharp edges
of harmattan winds against the rumbling weight
of May rainstorms.
I am the rainbow standing guard across
your path of storms.
Atsu I have died a hundred deaths for you.
Each time each night I wake up again and again
in that house we built upon the shores
with pools of troubled seas.

Come back home Agbenoxevi come back home

All all my peers now carry big babies on their back.
Still I carry mine in my heart. Sometimes in my loins.
And O she cries so much for you.

Come back home Agbenoxevi come back home

Kokui my young sister went away last Moon

at harvest time. She swallowed a tiny gourd seed
so now she carries a giant gourd in her belly
for Senyo our dying Chief's only living son.
Even Foli my mother's youngest child
now speaks in the broken voice of a man-child.
They say at the village school he goes
pinching the bigger girls on their wosowosos.
They always scream but they never report him.
And once the teacher caught him
he explained it was only a little test
to hear the difference in voice pitches
of teenage girls and teenage boys.
They let him off and now he comes boasting
he's man enough to handle a thousand meddling teachers.
He even talks to me of the swift madness there may be
in these words I give to winds for you.

    So come back home Agbenoxevi come back home

I have woven a hundred songs for you woven them
all into pillows for your wandering head of dreams.
For your bed I plucked feathers from peacock's pride.
Each midnight moonlight night I walk naked
to the crossroads towards the setting place of Sun
I lean against the firm bosom of our ancient baobab tree
I close my eyes I give your name to westbound winds.
And in careless abandon to joys there are in songs
I stretch my breast against the Moon's glory just
waiting to dance you home to your rainbow bed
where you and I may wrestle again all over again
in that old fertility game first played by gods
in the seedtime of our Earth.

I say today I stand naked beneath our baobab tree
watching your dreams running along the path of storms.
I will woo you yet with glories of the Moon while

our hunters break their tongues in strange whispers
of Moon deity at life's crossroads
keeping vigil for Sungod's homecoming
from ramblings across the skies through
thunder's gates and lightning's path
into house of fugitive dreams.

Come back home Agbenoxevi come back home

Come with me to your rainbow bed
where you and I shall wrestle again and again
all over again in that old fertility game
first played by gods in the seedtime of our Earth

Just come back home Agbenoxevi come back home.

Hohoe, 28 February 1978–Bloomington, 21 November 1979

∾∾∾∾∾∾∾∾∾∾∾∾∾∾∾∾∾∾∾∾∾∾∾∾∾∾∾∾∾∾
∾∾∾∾∾∾∾∾∾∾∾∾∾∾∾∾∾∾∾∾∾∾∾∾∾∾∾∾∾∾

PART THREE

MOMENTS

∾∾∾∾∾∾∾∾∾∾∾∾∾∾∾∾∾∾∾∾∾∾∾∾∾∾∾∾∾∾
∾∾∾∾∾∾∾∾∾∾∾∾∾∾∾∾∾∾∾∾∾∾∾∾∾∾∾∾∾∾

The Word

And so these worshippers of gorgon and moron
came into his home. He was away
in cornfields rehearsing the rain dance
in wake of wandering clouds . . .

To his kids they whispered things. Gave them
miracle drugs wrapped in arguments of sugar.
Gave them powdered milk in polythene bags.

He came back home with a harvest of
corn-cobs and honeycombs. His children
met him at the gates, singing hosayanas.
Their mother they said had gone
to the next and next village whispering The Word.

Bloomington, 22 April 1979

Of Fortune

We wield matchets against our own misdeeds
lopping away at mere shadows even where
our eyes refuse to look and the image flies
in mists of memory's dawn flying through
our soulsunsets beyond twilights into noon-
time dreams all marching down to harvest time of Earth.

The Housefly's fortune dance is
a going and a coming in a world that
runs runningforward runningbackwards . . .

Bloomington, 8 February 1979

And So

And so
I could go down in crouching postures
I could gather your woes your griefs
I could reach all out for that last
calabash of fresh palm-wine
and
go to sleep to sleep and sleep
sprawled upon the floor amid your tears . . .
But I would wake up before the squirrel's
search for a morning meal

I would pick up my hoe I would walk away from you . . .

Bloomington, 22 November 1978

Do not give too much of your love to me

Do not give too much of your love to me
I am the bird with voice of dreams
I bring the brief glory of wings upon the rays
Long ago I chose the rainbow for my soul

I am the bird in flight
the arrow through your night

Do not give too much of your love to me
Once the angels stole my cloth somewhere
upon the clouds in house of storms
Today I sweep the sky I leave footprints on thunderclouds
I spread the swift glory of wings upon the rays

O do not give too much of your love to me.

Bloomington, 14 April 1979

Murmuring

I met a tall broadchest
strolling down deepnight
with my fiancée in his arms
She passed me off for a third cousin
on her mama's side of a dried-up family tree

I nodded and walked away
murmuring unnameable things to myself

Legon, 10 May 1978

Singer Bird

The Singer Bird
comes in the wake of droughts
spreading a million beatitudes
over drooping fields of corn

They stand perplexed. These corn
with withered beards and dying babies
on their back nodding heads in solemn fear
for ancient skies with bone fingers
that bring the tears upon our old beleaguered world

O dance away and dance away
you lean High Priest in robes of coloured plumes
dance away and dance away and sway our world
to your slow rain dance of giant steps
across rainbows to sky-god's palace gates . . .

Bloomington, 9 September 1978

26

Some Say

They sold their shame
in old markets of new-found worlds
So now they sit on park benches
picking teeth and belching scorn
on wise restraints of the other side of things

Some say they are the by-products
of a civilised world
But their spokesman came to our court
of common lawlessness and nailed a note
to the chamber gate of the petty judge
He complains of certain big people in high and low places
who came to their hole the other night
and left in strange passion with threats
of setting state bulldogs to hunt them out
into deserts of our dream

And we who sit and watch these things
On whose right side do we stand?
Aha! On misjudgement day
On whose left side do we squat?

Verdict

The haggard man of old letters
nods his beard and smiles upon
the confidence of deep knowledge of all knowledge:

It's clear to me the way you people sing
that your tune your words could not
be traced to your father's father's gnomic chants
The grandmaster of course was an English peer
whose echo shakes the world to eternity

And I worry so much for our renegade self
Of course we are glad to be born to Universe.
But we'd love to leave our home address somewhere
specific directions about our house our home
our little place in a monstrous world
Yes we'd like to hang our own address
Up at the crossroads of this earth
lest the gods should one day
come looking us up in wrong places . . .

Hohoe, 2 June 1978

Newspeddler

Last night newspeddler told us how
at last they picked the venom from our voice
into stainless tubes well corked with seals of state

and we will glide through life with all sorrows
transformed into beatific visions of excess joy

So help us Dog!

Maamobi, Accra, 3 June 1977

Food for Ghosts

And they gathered our souls
into massive metal mortars and
with tall truncheons for pounding sticks
they are crunching our bones into sacrificial
food for their outraged ghosts
playing dirges on martial drums
to lend rhythm to the violence of their lust . . .

Legon, 10 May 1978

〜〜〜〜〜〜〜〜〜〜〜〜〜〜〜〜〜〜〜〜〜〜〜〜

PART FOUR

MY MAILMAN FRIEND WAS HERE

〜〜〜〜〜〜〜〜〜〜〜〜〜〜〜〜〜〜〜〜〜〜〜〜

89 Walnut Grove Courts
Indiana University
Bloomington, Indiana 47401
USA

16 April 1979

Kwakuvi, Kwakuvi,
Where was it heard before that
Afa's word-carriers should go astray
with the *du* still locked up in their jaws?
How come a voice vanished in skies
amid the whirl and twirl of iron birds?

I have often heard of hunger-eaten word-mongers
opening oracle bags all meant for diviners' eyes only
I have heard of careless hands and small-faced men
delivering *Afa*'s burdens to houses full of howling hounds
I have even heard of trickster gods breaking open
sealed secrets meant only for mortal eyes in Kodzogbe.
But I've never heard Kwakuvi's voice drying up in air
before it found my waiting ears across deserts
And yet somehow this too has come to be
The fact now stands your first *edu* has never found my ears.
I am so glad you've sent this second screaming one
And now I throw my *gumaga* and send you this *edu*:

Ekpo. They say *ekpo*.
The novice *Boko* searches his oracle-bag
and nods his head and says *ekpo*.
The *Dzogbana* searches and searches his oracle-mind
and shakes his head and says and says *ekpo ekpo*.
And so we know *ekpo*.

The thing that pushed Kwasi Sagbadre and
he did somersaults and fell into *avlime*
The thing that drove Dumega Domenyo
to hang himself in the baobab tree on our public square
though you send old Gbagbladza into inner rooms
of Dzogbana's oracle-mind, you'll search and search
you'll never find even Afi's skull.

And so Novinye Bokovi,
Let us not talk of sacrificial goats and immolator's knife
Let's not talk too loud of miracle-makers
with bags of gold hanging from their neck
One day at noon they'll open these bags and
find the gold is turned to sand.
They'll sit and eat their teeth.

For now let's talk only of how
our harvest gatherers sit on granary floors
with windfull baskets dreaming gathering
our laughters home to our children climbing
trees for brief glories of coming dawns.
Let's talk of how they sit leaning against
these winds, winnowing our memory in this
gentle breeze this stirring breath from
fertile river beds this breeze across deserts
across rainbows pouring through
the infancy of new cornfields.

They say the priest of feasts will come
one noon. He will proclaim the birth of joy.
So now we clean this house we burn the rubbish heaps
They say they say the gods are sanitary inspectors
They come searching water pots for mosquito eggs
They charge the family head for negligence of house keepers.

And so you say Alaisdair says **he has** to go?
Too bad he has to go. And yet **we understand**, don't we?
Don't they say Tagbatsutsu is always full of condolence
but he only takes a corpse to outskirts of the grave?
That he leaves a soul to count his final grains of salt?
But we'll remember his condolence with us
His memory we'll keep with others not so pleasant.

Did you say you want my mind on this
brave old world of the miracle-peddling race?
There is not much to give you now for *Legacy*.
I spend these seasons with my thoughts, revising
all old gospels according to *our* needs.

Of course there *are* wonders here. So much glory here.
They say it *is* a house of open dreams. Here man's confidence
measures the mind's capacity in terms as infinite
as the volume of our Earth's oceans. Here the dreams
of mythmakers are born anew at countdown time
on Kennedy's launching pads, and Adamu's spoilt children
walk the Moon in giant strides and trample Earth to dust.
Today they say the sky could *never* be the limit.
There are unbounded joys waiting they say
to embrace the dreamer's hopes and fears.

You know how much I yearn for pleasures of our Earth
But our ancient myths of memory keep holding back
the burst of passion's sway.
All around the edges of these joys I think I see
the smiles of witches casting lots for a holocaust of screams
I think I read these faint patterns of snake progress
in *husago* drums and their graceful dance of
death even where they insist it's all a dance of life.

Of course I may be wrong. Thank Dogs I may be wrong!

32

But my old diviner-friend, again I pray
Let's not talk too loud of miracle-makers
with bags of gold hanging from their neck
One day at noon we'll find
the gold is turned to sand.
They'll sit and eat their teeth.

Salaam alekum
Enye Akakpo Afagbedzi.

Bloomington
6 June 1979

Old De Boy Kodzo
I write you long long tam, I no dey hear from you.
I say me I go write you somting small again.
Dem tell me say you too you come for Varsity
Me I say tank Gods! Old De Boy too icome for where
dem say all de small peoplo mas come and make dem
big peoplo. But lak I say som tam before de sodza peoplo
come bloody ma mauf, too much book ino go make your
pikin belly full. But I sabi say your own concrete head
be too too fool.
Make you go hask Plofessor Kesedovo
Haskam say na which peoplo tief our corn?
First, igo tell you somting for som sakabo man
dem callam Kominizimu. Den igo tell you somting too
for som lie lie tiefman dem callam Demoklashi.
De big bookman go spiti im rotten salava for your face
and make som long long talk about cockloach and housefry.
Igo gib you somting dem callam Footunotu.
Na dis one go say:

    Accorling to Disguintis Plofessor
       so so and so, and so and so,
    Accorling to meditasion espelmentasion and
       sciefitic obsavasion invastigasion,

33

Accorling to hleflence page so, palaglaf so so and so,
   articre one-and-half minus tree-one-qwata,
Accorling to accorling and accorling . . . .
   ibi akuko didi kakra.

Now make you hol im beard make you haskam again:
   So, Plofessor, na which peoplo tief we corn?
Igo smal kakra igo pull im beard igo say:
   To be continua . . .

O yah to be continua
So we too we dey and we go continua.
As for we dem say we be simpel peoplo o
And so na how we go do?
Ah! me Bro, make I continua for you paa.

Na dis tam dem tell me say
De zombi peoplo go take all dat useless cedi
Dem go trowam all for bola. I say tank Gods!
Dem go trow all dem useless cedi for bola buuummm!
Den I say again O Gods Awuradi Nyankopong!
Why? Why you no collet all dees useless kalabule peoplo
and trow dem too for bola? Why? O Gods why you let all
dees nyamanyama peoplo halahala ma peoplo lak so?
Na God too I tink say idie long long tam ago ago.
Or lak idey for up, na im too perlaps go say:
   To be continua.

Wallahi! Tallahi! Bismillahi! Rrahmani-Rrahimi!
                    Salaam alekum
                    Ibi mea. Your Vagabond Broda
                    Kofi Abunuwas Abodzise.

Kokueee!
The mailman brought your voice a few breathings ago.
Again I remember our dead brother who sang a dirge
for a season of moon ethics, a dirge of a new warrior race
with fierce moustache and brief command.
And O how soon the diviner's chants
outrun the cynic's cheeky laughs!
You know our people sing and still
they sing of things that shouldn't be:

Amekee du avanu gagbe ava mayi?

These warrior lords gathered at dawn
in the elephant grass behind our Chief's palace.
They ate the feast of war. Now they announce
the war cry was a joke. But they beat
war drums they sang war songs in a victory dance
for a battle never fought, not ever won nor even lost.

The drums will never burst. These drums will wail
and groan. They will boom and vow and curse.
In better times the Panther's warrior dance
was the final step in a long sequence of martial deeds.
The infant cub never took his time to learn.
He went and stole War Mother's gown of charms.
He thinks the dance of war was a dance of children's game.

A divination outruns the brief logic of guns.
Our warrior lords defeat their own victory.
With their right feet in mid-air
the spirit of war has taken his dance over.
They violated the sequence of the dance, so the unrehearsed
are tumbling down from weight of stolen feasts.

Who with Panther's grace can tread the Earth
    so firm without a boast?
Who to weave the final regal step in this
    long sequence of royal dreams?

So long ago we lost the count counting time
in changing beats of new and new drummers
We now must push these fumbling ones to
totter their hunt to a final final fall.
Let someone pick their bastard cub and teach him well
the first of steps in ancient rhythmic moves
across warfields into harvest time of Earth.

They who eat the feast of war and beat
war drums for a joke, must pay with blood
in the peace time of their soul's harvest.
            Lala salama.
            Kofi Gbedzidzavu.

                              Bloomington
                            10 June 1979

Koku leee!
Woke up late this day feeling slightly stupid
from too much booze at a late night groove.

First of all the newsman came: no new news,
just full-page ads offering the world for sale.
I must decline these good offers though they urge
I could have it all on credit card on Master Charge.

Then my mailman friend on his daily drives
wondering why I always get so many mails
across deserts across oceans all the way from Africa.
I explain I have people. Lots of good people.

(Some bad ones too!) O yes, I have people
Though I sit down here alone. In this walnut grove
watching snow-and-thunderstorms whirling through
and around my trailer court. In this place of blooms
where once they say our Indianman
paid the cruel price of too much love for his Earth
and fought his life to Death's doorsteps.

My mailman friend was here. Brought your two letters
each urging me to stay and read the books,
not try too hard to come back home this first summer
only to leave again too soon
But I have this great hunger for home.
Not all the honey of this promise land nor all
MacDonald's hamburgers and Wendy's hero sandwiches
nor all the cold turkeys of Thanksgiving
nor the Colonel's thirty million Kentucky fried chickens
may ever fill this yawning soul of mine.

You talk to me of books, Koku? O well and hell
they have them all down here: a monster home
all full and fool of books. Half of these are
mere verbiage or hot dog shit. Half the other half
are strict matters of cold Theory. O yes, the scholar's
pride is now become the fierce logic of swift and violent
    thought:
Analytical categories. Hyperpothetical constructs.
Functions. Paradigms. Parallel structural theses.

Then they twist the arm of Fact to hold imagined Truth.

I must admit there is some good stuff here as well.
Hardened facts of Earth sticking out in neat logic
of doomed prophets of Truth, angry fellows growing
pretty hungry in a world bargained away to master thoughts
of new gurus without a god without belief in the mystery
of the rainbow's dance across our skies into planets in our soul.

And Maxwell talks so well of the usefulness of the useless,
mythmakers who grind their fame upon our skull across
our collarbone, mythmakers and history's pawnbrokers.

They ask so much, so much more than ever I can hope
to have to give. You know my credit stands so so low
with all our banking gods: you'll find my poverty in full
colour on tall billboards across the skies of old Wall Street.

But in the wake of all our new nightmares, our haunting gift
of death of faith, I would choose the coward's hope of life,
choose those galloping dreams of our land over swift logic
of post-industrial thought:

>   the certainty of the coroner's seal
>   the irregular flow of welfare cheques
>   the house in flames insurance claims
>   the nursing home and Old People's Rhymes

I did not tell you this before. No need to raise an alarm
where nothing could be done. But I fell on ice I broke my wrist.
Just walking through the wintry cold to their warmer house of
    books.
I tripped I fell I broke my wrist.
In the medicine house of the miracle-making race
they trapped the image of my bones broken beneath
the skin beneath the flesh. But they have no herb to urge
the health of broken bones. And all these tedious winter weeks
I sit and watch my hand still trapped inside these castle walls
And I shake my head in sweet memory of a far-off land
with our secret store of miracle herbs.
Salaam. Kofi.

Akofa, Akofa,
They say you came back home some ten Tuesdays ago
at 8.10pm. What shame I was not there to take you in.
But you'll be at home among the people you will find.
If they're not your papa's people, they'll be your mama's
    people.
You'll find you'll have more people than ever you can count.
Indeed one of your granduncles would call himself:

    Thousand Thousand I have Thousand Thousand
    people.
    So what does it count that I look so poor?

Your mama says there is a mystery in your eyes.
Your uncle Koku says he can tell from your eyes
you're happy you're here. But I cannot see your eyes
in this photo you have sent. Your eyes are closed but
I can tell you're not asleep. And is that a smile
or a little frown you carry on your face?

Perhaps Akua will ask you about me. Well, just tell her
I'm fine thank you and thank you all again and again.
Sometimes your friends will say your papa is a rogue
and he is a travelling man. They'll say may be his mama
ate dog feet upon his head. You see how little children
sometimes say bad bad things about their friends' papas
and their mamas too. Just tell your friends they may be
telling lies and lies. You can say you know some bad bad things
about their papas too and their mamas too, but you'll
never say such bad bad things about no one's papa.
And if they ask you where on earth I am, just point
up to the sky. Say your papa caught a rainbow on his farm
and now he's gone to give it back to God. But he told someone

to tell someone to bring you promises. He's coming home next time.

I have a gift for you from Moon.
Stay well, Akofa. Give a smile to Akua and to Mama.

Papa.

~~~~~~

PART FIVE

MOKPOKPO
~~~~~~

They Hunt the Night

They have sought to put us away like
memories of a bad marriage of youth
But like wounds from naughty childhood days
We leave a perpetual scar upon
the forehead of their joy.

We are the dog who caught the game
but later sat beneath the table
over bones over droppings from the mouth.
In gentle tones the master talks of angels
coming down with gifts for God's children
Still we sing of ghosts who would not go to hell.
They hunt the night from cottage door to palace gate
knocking with boney skinny hands, scaring away
God's own children from playing fields at heavens gate.

So they seek to muzzle our howls, to chain our anguish
to their gates of hell. May be tomorrow they will
sweep us all into garbage cans with other testimonials
of their greed. But on wings of flames we'll rise and
float across their joys and rain rumours of blood
upon their festive dreams: Rumours Dreams Blood.

Bloomington, 15 October 1978

Long Distance Runner

From Frisco once
we drove across the wide yawn of the breezy bay
to the Oakland home of Mike who fixed
a memorial dinner for his years among our people

They call for song and I sing the story
of our wounds: the failures and betrayals
the broken oaths of war leaders grown smooth
with ease of civil joys

They laugh they clap they call for more

For a change just for a little change I sing
your dirge about their land's defeat in the beauty
of her dawn: the ghost of Harlem standing guard
across their bridge of mirth their launching pad of dream and
    myth.
I sing also your long lament for grand Geronimo
Amerindian chieftain who opened his heart a bit too wide
the lonely horseman who now perhaps only may be
still rides his old stallion across their dream their myth
forever riding his memory among mirages along eternities
reserved for him among snowfields spread across the breast
of the Earth this Earth and all his Earth.

Halfway through your songs I see the folly
and the wisdom of our choice in the cold stare
the shifting look in the eyes of our hosts our very kind hosts

Who are we to throw back at a man the image of things
he strove so hard to burn to ashes in history's bonfires?

We know there is an agony in waiting for the long distance
    runner
who breaks the finisher's line for the judges to declare he

jumped the starter's gun stepped upon some other
runner's toes threw him off balance and off the race

And what is a race, Cousin, without the rules
without other runners?

But leave him alone leave him alone to his
glory looming large above his olive dreams.

Bloomington, 23 November 1978

Fugitive Dreams

Sons of the SunGod
we woo the Moon
along the frigid zones
of our fugitive dreams
seeking our night across
the backyard of the skies

They rode our dawn across
thornfields of the centuries
riding riding our memories
into snowstorms through
tornado bowls across
blizzards into caves of ice

They stripped us naked
in the market place of gods
so now we wear a gown of flames
and spread mirages across
deserts and prairie fields
gathering the harvest
of their dreams into
snowballs for a game of peace of war
with Moonchildren on fields of storm

Still they ride riding our rainbows
across graveyards and battlefields
of history's stupid wars
mythmaking our world from
wayward dreams of fallen gods

Let me borrow the voice of silverman
and sing of mirages in these deserts of our soul.

Bloomington, 11 October 1978

Atta

Your whispers came
thundering through those old thornfields
and the lightning from your voice
quenched the triumph in my eyes

Memories away from home we scampered through
death traps of Niger area in flight away from
screams of Lagos City from old Ibadan stalking
through the dawn we circled round Kaduna down
to Jos and up again to Zaria Kano Sokoto coming
through Ogbomosho Ilorin Jebba Kontagora

I wonder what it was we were looking all for what?

We were among forgotten fields of Dan Fodio's jihads
when voices came falling on our peace chanting
destoolment riots far back home on troubled shores.
Caught off-guard in mid-pleasure
we knelt upon bridgehead at Nigerbend
we saw eternity crawl over ample breasts of earth

we changed our mind about what the prophets said
about the ultimate fate of Earth of Man

Through doomsday from creation night
we may sit upon these rocks and watch
the Fulani cattle's dance of grace on
graves of ancient kingdoms
But your thirst for new desires still
beckoned to us across the skies and I shall
see you off at the next bus-stop of life
Then I will go back home and wait knowing
some day you too should make your sentimental
homecoming and you will find me sitting firm
in the middle of our piece of Earth leaning against
the withered family tree with a borrowed umbrella
unfurled above my thoughts still nursing wounds
from thorns planted in our thoughts by those
whose memory we laid to rest long long ago

Atta, Atta, at what point in our ramblings
did we miss that narrow pass across stormtime
into jubilee halls of Hell?

Ibadan-Zaria-Jos, 17–19 July 1977

Our Fortune's Dance

The raw energy of a certain rolling stone
came rumbling through our well-carved dreams.
Our master hunters had climbed up trees
to pluck berries. They fell in love with Moon.
So *adekploviawo* must wield matchets
and face the panther's wrath.

My singer friend has sent a song of how
today the land is ruled by monstrous things
with huge dense beards. They had no head.

My people how soon again in our hive
shall we swarm around our honeycomb?

I still recalled that day our hunter-bees
came at dawn and did our fortune's dance.
We could not catch the scent they said
they brought upon their gun muzzles.
We drank too much of the sweetened wine
of alien royal palms. Too much of it we drank.
So now we lose our weight against
the giddy force of the season's thunderstorms.

Someone took our Mother-Queen away.

Our people how soon again in our hive
shall we swarm around our honeycomb?

Bloomington, 14 June 1979

The Panther's Final Dance

And so the Hippo seeks
our stool of thorns our crown of thunder?
Let him beware the final dance of
soothsayers who now become our praise gatherers.

Once the Thunder ruled this land our home
He picked a clique of trickster gods
for councilmen and ministers of state
And Thunder lost his voice one
harmattan dawn at whirlwind time.

And Panther came in flash of guns
smote down the rule of demi-semi-dogs.
Our bookmakers revised the word erased
the curse on breakers of the rule of natural laws

And Panther grew too fond of spoils of civil peace.
He crawled around munching chicken coaxing goats
to come witness his wedding feast for butterfly ladies.

But a strange passion came upon the children
of the land: They wielded blunt matchets.
They clipped the Panther's claws. Somehow
they forgot the Panther's teeth. Now our
caretaker gods are sending back the lame Panther
to his place of birth in the forest zone. They say
his name has been erased from the big game hunter's scroll.
And yet somehow they too forget his teeth,
and then of course his feet.

And if the Hippo seeks
our stool of thorns our crown of thunder
Let him beware the final dance of praise gatherers.

Bloomington, 20 May 1979

48

From ChristianBorg to UssherFort

(From UssherFort to ChristianBorg)

So we broke our vows across our shoulderblades
opening our arms again to gather new fortunes
from winds born of storms. And you will be
our ferryman across the confluence of dreams

They say you have good guts to well digest
that strange madness in which glories are cooked
for men of state. That is good beyond
the reach of arguments. But of all men
we have and may be will ever have,
a breach of faith from you will be beyond
the reach of pleas and screams.
You who made a name sharpening your tongue
splitting open the wrapped-up shame of false deities
Beware the slippery stairs to heavens gate

Come take us through these dreamfields of our land.
We will gather again the unfinished harvests
of lost seasons and I will be the old choirboy with
a basketful of songs for our festivals of peace.

But if you too should leave ungathered
all the bounties of our dreams
We would hang a thousand curses round your neck.
Some say you would spare yourself
these ungovernable passions of makers of the law
the sudden disease that comes to mar
the holiday joys of ex-statesmen and
cuts short the hopes of their heirs.

Bloomington, May 1979

49

Allahu Akbar! . . . Allahu Akbar!

The Shah

Somewhere somewhere a hurricane
whirls across some palace gates
gathering away the glory of the King
with his velvet robes drying in the Sun.

Children release their kites into eternities
sending dreams to fairy godmothers
with hopes to grow some day to fly
to where only kites may reach today.
In the wake of a storm the King's kinsmen
are retesting all foundations of their faith.
They erected a monument of words
for the infinite beauty of their dream
Today they wake up at dawn and find
their sacred cock has flown away to sea

The sacrificial ram now runs amok
with a trail of blood across the palace gates.

Bloomington, 9 December 1978

Iran

So the newsmen talked of how he stands
alone and away in alien fields standing
firm against the giddy whirl of western winds

By their own logic of what
and how the wider world must see
they spoke of a strange madness
a massmadness of simple-minded men women
whose faith mistook the sophistry of civilised guns
for a game of toys scattered in the sand.

50

Devotees must fall with prayers on their lips.

But now the newsmen say the good old King
has taken a vacation trip, hovering above
some alien fields with a gold casket
of Persian soil under his captain's seat.
Once so long the pilot of his single destiny
across and away from cold currents
that drown his people's dreams
today he stears his flight away from home
from death from birth rebirth of old nightmares.

And flowers hung from gun muzzles where once
often blood flowed and still will flow again
and again into streams that wash the guilt
away from the old palace where now this caretaker
invokes a sudden right to ancient thrones in fields of Oil.

Bloomington, 4 February 1979

The Ayatollah

And the voyager comes back home
to his broken house of storms

They say he has excess baggage
of faith in righteousness of ancient dreams:
 Allahu akbar! . . . Allahu akbar! . . .

Renegade

From memory of the rioting mob
they hooked him out
for dishonourable mention in official bulletins
His name they nailed
to the upas tree on our public square

The crows will come and peck
at the vision in his eyes
But the harvest of his dreams
will not belong to the vampire

Our doves will come gather his words
into secret barns of souls
whose insurance against decrees of death
will not expire before the third coming

From hideouts in carnage groves
the vultures smell rumours
of blood flowing in open fields

They purge themselves against the feast of rot
But grief shall be the only testimonial for their greed.

Maamobi, Accra, 3 June 1977

Kingmaker

From far across the skyline came the voice
that chained our thunder to the clouds

I will roost among your murmurs
and watch the Kingmakers
making destoolment logic
against the stool they made
only a little while ago.

Nana holding on to his sandals
weaving a knot of words for a guest linguist:

> Tell them, Demaso,
> to weigh the meat with eyes
> to beware rejecting a thigh for an arm
> See, Madeso, see the lame Panther
> plays at marbles with Duiker's child
> and Duiker insists on revision of the rules
> to ban the use of paws
>
> Sodema, there is a rumbling in the air
> Call the priests to read this blank in our stare.

Legon, 16 January 1977

Rush-Hour in Soul-City

Standing beneath your silk cotton at noon
I watch these little little ones
searching your village sands for lost pesewas
glancing across your empty market square
to the lean woman in noonday sun
selling hot beanstew with cold cornbread
and
from rush-hour in soul-city
memories come crowding through our world

Once upon a time at a point of time
and place in soul-city
we were whirlpools and whirlwinds and whirlthoughts
flooding earthspace and airspace and mindspace
we were voices and echoes and waves
weaving rainbows and rhythms across the twilight zone
we were dreams sending moonbeams
along timewaves to other rainbows
standing guard at heaven's other gate.

It is rush-hour in soul-city
and on shores of eternity
ghosts are doing a ceremonial dance
at rebirth of new heroes

and here on earth we stand in flesh
to bargain with death over life's remnants
a widow sells cold cornbread
to outlive her husband's last harvest
an orphan searches sands for lost kobos
to kill the last hunger of youth

and still on shores of eternity
ghosts are doing a ceremonial dance
at rebirth of lost heroes
who
once upon a time at a point of time
and place in soul-city
were whirlthoughts and whirlwinds and whirlpools
flooding mindspace and airspace and earthspace
they were voices and echoes and soundwaves
weaving rainbows and rhythms across their twilight zone

We will again we will be dreams sending moonbeams
along timewaves to those rainbows
standing guard at heaven's other gate.

Hohoe, 1 January 1978

Pan Am 188

New York-Dakar-Accra

Today we speak these fears using past tense
And now I come a chief mourner
at obsequies for bad kinsmen.
Maybe it's good to know
the men you loved and then hated
should one day go to hell and give you back your joy.

I shall stand before the gods
and plead guilty to a certain callousness:
such terrifying joy burying kinsmen
with no sudden feel of loss, no tears nor emptiness.

So often in our time we've lived as
orphans in our home, picking crumbs from garbage heaps
cracking kernels with our teeth while our late uncles
stood by asking stupid questions about bad harvests and
negligence of old Nyame and rainmakers. They even
talked some jazz of technical aid and capital investment codes.

It's touchdown time and I see the concrete road
our Uncle Kwame built for his murdered dreams
to ride upon into harbours of our new anthems.
Now I guess I must distort my face for the mourner's
    homecoming.

8–9 July 1979

Sunbird

for Adele

They say the orphan may not die without
    a taste of harvest joys
Today your praise name laughs like west winds
    among our cottonfields
I found you in that walnut grove playing games
    with Moonchildren

Rainbows of Fall now play like glow worms
    in shadows of thunderstorms
You and I are grandchildren of SunGoddess
Here we stand naked in fields of snow
drinking pollen from breasts of shooting stars
But soon too soon my ticket will be here
and then I'll have to go

I may never find your voice among our harvest joys
But I'll search the songs of our people for echoes
of your laughter bursting through a million orgasms
    into Adamu's desecrated apple grove
My memory shall roll like sand dunes across those
cottonfields where once our Sunbird wove pillows
for the anguish of our Soul.
    Pay my joy to John and Kay.

Bloomington, 14 November 1979

ELEGY FOR THE REVOLUTION

To the memory of
    The Revolution that went astray
and for
    Those who refused to die

Libation

Avakpata-Avazoli deliver me
deliver me across my joy
unto the kindness of The Vampire
My blood may quench her thirst for other souls
Let not this blood clot upon your love
I am strangling my joy within the bosom of your peace

The rotten soul of my festive years
is now an orphan to my bastard joy
My laughter congeals within the warmth of
my heart and Oh if death were not but a myth
I could slaughter my life upon your altars
This eternity of my penance
Torments the divinity of my soul
with the fierceness of noon madness

deliver me   deliver me
across my joy unto the kindness of The Vampire

Legon, 20 January 1977

My Last Testament

Adonú Adokli
Dancer – Extra – Ordinary
who threw dust into Master Drummer's eyes
so you've gone the way of flesh
danced on heels in a backwards
loop into the narrow termite home
Whatever befalls the panther in the jungle
The leopard would not forget about the hunt

The dreams we placed among the thorns
are still unhatched
Those debts we owe our orphan clan
are yet unpaid
and you – you –
Whatever befalls the leopard in his ambush
The panther could not betray the spirit of the hunt

Here at the haunted outskirts of life
I've crouched for a season
watching your rainbows dissolving into mist
Now I smell thunders
loading their cannons with furies of storms
my horizons grow blurred with
shivering images of all our old visions
a holocaust hangs upon the clouds
threatening remembrance of life's purpose
with a blank sheet of doubts
Now I gnash my teeth
bite my lips in a sudden resolve
to invoke grandfather's spirit name

Kátáko Gakó
Old Mad – One says
he captured King Cobra's neck with naked hands
Yah! Kúmasí the Fearless Ghost
wrestles a soul from jaws of Death
Come, blood of spirits
Daze my eyes to fear
I toss these rising doubts to thunder
and stagger back into my soul, still
holding firm onto this growing confidence
this piece of our broken covenant
Whatever befalls the panther in the desert
The leopard would not forget the jungle war

Legon, 16 November 1976

Oath of Destiny

they perch upon the parapets, these renegade sons of our soil,
hurling profanities at the pedlars of decency
pouring vulgarity into the council chambers of the moralists:

> You cover your rotten sores with borrowed
>   velvet robes, coat your diseased teeth with
>   stolen gold, and walk our corridors with
>   the Bible on your tongue, selling the gospel
>   for weekly collections of silver.

To

> whose dog did you give your shame, that
>   you dare offer the holy sacrament with
>   illicit wine, and bread baked with
>   corn swindled from our starving pagan peasants?

> Your mouth you wash thrice a day, but
>   your bowels you never purge, and
>   our air stinks with the stench from your guts.

> WE no longer can wait for the Second Coming
>   of YOUR Christ
> nor for the Judgement Day appointed
>   by your God
> *Chukwu* has grown impatient with the unlimited
>   patience of *Jehovah*, and can no longer
>   await the pleasure of Jesus

> Before the High Council of the Supervising Deities of
>   this soil of broken oaths and widowed virgins,
>   we summon you

We the little great-great-grand-children of
    Oduduwa and *Obatala*
We charge you
charge you with innumerable counts of
despoiling our virgins and killing our little joys
we challenge you

By all the thunders of *Xebieso*
By all the incurable infirmities of *Sakpana*
We swear
We swear to post copies of the Judgement
    to your God, who is in Heaven
    Whose address we shall look up
    in the opening chapters of the
    Holy Bible, Unrevised Version.

Back to Memory

    running away from memory
    searching for reasons to die

You will go and come come and go
hoping to break these chains of life
but your renegade mind will ride
your degenerate flesh across
fields littered with corpses of dreams
you dreamt once upon a hope
when the soul's desires burst in
upon strongholds of Hell, blew out
hellfire with a breath of mirth
long before the flash of lightning
smote down hellgate, letting loose

the thousand fiends that today
you pursue across deserts and battlefields
sending your mind

running away from memory
searching for reasons to die

The searchlights of your mind's day –
dreams are trapped by long shadows
of life, shoved off the cliff of memories
Your paralysed soul somersaults onto
rubber rocks that bounce you back to life
and you will mount the clouds
to the house of storms where
guardian demons relieve the mind
of its useless burden of death
They will send you back to memory
Make you rich with reasons not to die

Legon, 6–7 March 1976

Soul in Birthwaters

Suite for the revolution

Our Birth-Cord

> a piece of meat lost in cabbage stew
> it will be found   it will be found

If we must die at birth, pray
we return with our birth-cord still uncut
our oneness with Earth undefiled

Last night on the village square a man
bumped into my conscience and cursed
our god. I refused to retort, knowing
how hard it is for man to wake a man
from false slumber
Our conscience would not be hurt
by threats of lunatics

> a pinch of salt lost in cabbage stew
> it will be found   the tongue will feel it out

We heard their cries but thought of dogs
and ghosts. Ghosts gone mad at dogs
who would not give our village a chance
to sleep, to dream
Now they say we have to die
These brand-new men gone slightly drunk
on public wine they say we have to die

Yet if we must die at birth, pray
we return with our birth-cord still uncut
our name still to be found in the book of souls

Across the memory of a thousand agonies
our death shall gallop into the conference hall of a million hopes
a lone delegate at reshuffling of destinies

    a piece of hope lost in public tears
    it will be found   it will be found

And if we must die at birth, pray
we return with –
But we were not born to be killed
by threats of lunatics
The maimed panther is no playmate for antelopes

12 August 1975

Radio Revolution

Again this dawn our Radio
broke off the vital end of sleep

Revolution! . . . Devolution! . . . Resolution!

grab a razor-sharp matchet
and step onto the paths of war

Across our yard I disturbed a courtship of
the dogs. They barked and backed away

through streets to all familiar walks
through maze of slums to armed barracks
of peace. Where? Where?
old peasant with hoe in hand, I
seek Revolution. Where is Revolution?
young veteran with blood across blue eyes, I
knew of no Revolution, but I
met Revolt limping down this road
chased by a howling herd of armed jackals

down this road down this road
to the market square where an only
pig searching for a morning meal
took me for a moving lump of flesh
and charged at me charged at me
with fangs sharpened by hunger's despair

I slashed her into two, wiped her
blood upon
                    her head

down this road   down this road
to Dependence Square seeking Revolution
I found a lone symbol for Peace
a nameless bronze warrior with empty
gun pointing earthwards doing homage
to earth goddess

The school-boy newspeddler leans against
a smile tells of how he came and found my doors
open my inner rooms unguarded in the dawn

I was out my dear
I was out seeking Revolution

Our Revolution, Sir? It's here in these
dailies. The headlines display it:

THE REVOLUTION – NOT A CONCERT PARTY

The photographs confirm it:

Statesmen at State Banquets
Proposing a toast to the health of State:
LONG LEAVE THE REVOLUTION!!!

Legon, 5–7 March 1976

On My Honour

a streetwalker emerges unhurt from
a drunken brawl
raising broken bottles to stars

i never stole a brother's girl
i could never steal a comrade's wife
candidate for new honours
my hands are clean
though my toes are soiled with
a little mess from our dunghill of common crimes

This sister came over at noon
holding a plea to her bosom
The revolution had drafted her
man into the national service corps
He was out in the field campaigning
for redemption of our souls
They shot him in the waist
She drafted me into service for her people
And we are one people with a single destiny

The revolution swings to a
pause at central durbar grounds
There are laurels and medals for new heroes

Wheta, 5 September 1976

Soweto

let us accept the curse prescribed
by the good old lord
preach it a 1000 times
according to lessons read
by voices in the whirlwind

gospel confronts gospel
high-tension power-line
connects their various truths
the preacher creates a new
Gospel According to His Needs

we will make heroes out of streetboys
train felons into statesmen
now world assemblies deal in lies
let us recruit liars for diplomats

Legon, 29 September 1976

HouseBoy

a young revolutionary lays ambush in my thoughts
firing sound bombs
into colonial barricades

my memory bumps
into the silence of
his 70-year-old
HouseBoy
he serves champagne in panelled living rooms
retreats at night to a toy
mud-hut with a bamboo bed
swallows a glass of liquid flames
turns his dreams loose
upon his private agonies

The dreams of Fanon's wretched of the earth
condense into storms in our morning sky
and
The burden of our guilt
hangs heavy upon our harvest joys

old memories discharge poison
arrows into banquet
halls where invalid souls
gather celebrating a treaty of
peace between aggrieved conscience
and crimes against the self

Legon, 29 September 1976

Ghosts

a thousand ghosts haunt our soul in birth waters
this life would drown in blood
hammer falls on anvil of
this head, calabash cracks
scattering braindrops on pathways
offering a broken tale to passers-by

watch revolutions of worlds
load guts of goats with power of
bulls, the fools we were
we would seek refuge on wings of their visions
deserting the dream we placed among the thorns

they stole our sleep in a daylight siege
and in our brief madness we
exchanged lullabies for anguished cries

we were all away on the farm
when prowlers of night
sneaked into our pillows
oh they would ambush our sleep
and strangle our dream
the vampires! I saw them
they know I saw them when
father sent me home to fetch a little salt

My voice my voice they seek after my voice!
Do not put me to sleep my people.

Legon, 31 December 1976

Dogs

The nose once said to the ear
all I ask of life
is just a little breath

Madman in the market-place
Let me be
only a madman in your market-place
I would howl and howl all day
but only to remind these
ghosts you're supposed to be in hell

Some people are cursing my dogs for
howling through their sleep
How would they know of
strange shadows
prowling among their sheep?

Legon, 31 December 1976

Finale for Evil Ones

revolutions
                    subversions
tribunals
                    confessions

The heart of our father is
an open casket of free pardons
The ache of our jaw would be appeased with
a sacrificial extraction of raging canine teeth

Teeth of gold are false
but they are decorations to
a mouth fouled by belch of ill-digested feasts

A man in the witness box swears the cross
tells of how his blood-brother
sharpened a dozen new matchets
swore to shave heads of state
he claimed had grown unwieldy on our shoulder

By night we went By night we came
The big drum sounds a finale for evil ones
They say they sat in secret groves
plotting the death of infant hopes

at life's roundabout ancestral deities
prepare a feast for returning souls

in bedchambers of state a crown witness
avoids questions in his women's eyes
the unspoken doubts on his children's lips

Wheta, 4 September 1976

Elegy for the Revolution

a feverish psyche gropes for an
eye in the shrines of Xebieso
the armoured hope lies exposed
to wrath of thunderbolts

These feet have kissed the sands of many shores
Today they lay in cramps, crushed by revolving wheels of
State
This heart has felt the warmth of love, throbbed to
beats of a thousand joys let loose upon a festive world
Today it is a husk of corn blown before the burning grass

The Revolution violates a devotee. Beware
Beware the wrath of thunderbolts
The agonised thoughts of a detainee translate
our new blunders into nightmares of blood & sweat:
    whips slashing through tender skins, broken bones
    collapsing to floors of cells, tortured moans
    bursting through concrete walls
    tearing through clouds and skies
    They seek refuge in house of storms
    and a sad conscience clears a path
    for poison arrows of gods of wrath

From sheltered yards of our righteousness
we watched the loading of an atom bomb
with a doubt on our lips, our cheeks
still blown with mirth of nights of revelry
our drunken ease forgetful of speed of light and sound:
    The muzzled heat of Hiroshima bursts into
    sudden flames, burns our laughter into
    screams. Our crippled mirth wades through
    streams of blood, groping for memories of
    feasts flowing down turbulent gulfs
    half-filled with discarded blue-prints for
    a revolution gone astray into
    arms of dream merchants.

Legon, 28 February 1976

Dance of Death

Let us celebrate our
death by firing squads
To beats of martial strains
let us link our arms
on these public fields of blood
teach our feet to do the dance of death

Now there is still
some laughter in our souls
our feet with skill
will teach our pride to do the dance of death

The birth of a new nation
calls for sacrifice of souls
and our hearts are filled with
a passion for life by baptism of death

The growls of lions
are muffled by mumblings of thunder
The poise of panthers
baffled by flashes of flaming skies
The antelope passes through
on its peace mission to the little stream of life

Our minds have laboured in vain
preparing blue-prints for revolutions of peace

In this final hour of our triumph
let us celebrate our
death by firing squads
On these public fields of blood
let us link our arms
and teach our feet to do the dance of death

It is at the place of the dance
that elbow meets elbow
It is on the field of execution
that death embraces life
This is our ritual celebration
of marriage of death to life
The throb of mortal hearts
prepare our feet for the dance of cosmic love
The dance of death is a dance of grace

Put the rhythm to the loom
Weave new tapestries for our gliding feet
This rhythm grows too urgent for our peace
splitting our souls among a thousand desperate loves
The dance of death is a dance of grace
Give us back those old drummers
Give them back those broken drums with nasal twangs
Call them here call the owners of our town
Bring them stools to sit in state and watch
our feet in this final glide across our twilight zone

The birth of a new world
demands a little sacrifice of souls
and our hearts are filled with
a passion for life by baptism of death

The god of creation rambles
through the ruins of broken worlds
and
The process of reconstruction
is also
A process of demolition

Wheta, 4–11 September 1976

New Birth-Cords

You sit searching raindrops
for tears of thunder gods
harvesting shooting stars
in hope to rebuild comets
that strayed into uncharted milky-ways

You detain trade winds and bargain
for purified curses of rebel deities

That cloudy noon before
joy-maker's brief madness
say that mid-day night
when you stood upon the banks of our humanity
and peered into our soul
what was it you saw
what indeed did you see
that today you are a ghost
haunted by crippling memoirs of years
and tears ago, unmoved by vows of rebirth
and oaths to weave new birth-cords
into honeymoons of coming resurrections?

Mean souls, unable to bear
the bruise of life's strictures
snatch at false deaths built of flimsy martyrdoms
Are you one of these?
seeking to make of your soul a sacrificial
sheep on the defiled altar of a nation's dreams

The world our world is not worth dying for

a life is dearer than a wreath of tears
a nation may lay for a soul
All this talk of redeemers and sacrifice
of souls is a trap by rogues
a mesh to ensnare unwary souls
do them in for extra days of joy

Do not brother die for a myth

Legon, December 1975

Upon the Harvest Moon

Between seasons of burning grass
and harvest moons, there are reasons
for jokes, Tuglo. And while
our whet-stones wait for hoes to come
while our baskets sleep old burdens
away into dream markets of harvest joys
Let us give these rising doubts to thunder
And peddle in harmless jokes

Remember remember that last hunt of childhood
how we dug for rats, probed our thumb
into python's jaws. He didn't bite
though we died a moment's death
He did not bite. The snake god's wish

They say Akofa your first love, she
who taught you dreams of maturing
left on your bed a pillow filled with sighs, she
Akofa of our dying chief's newest marriage bed
They say she's flown away to Nogokpo
with a curse on her womb. And
the thunder god demands a ram
with

     dangling
              testicles
akeden   keden
The ram's testicles.   They
                       dangle
Dangle
teasing barren maidens
with reserved manhood

Once upon a hope a man sold his wretched
heritage, trekked into the rainbow,
made potfuls of splendour, pawned the splendour
for gold, bought passage aboard comets
for excursions into eternal deliriums
In dream markets of remnant milky-ways
he exchanged his last droppings of gold
for a handful of cowries, returned,
bought back his place of birth
for the rights to a convenient grave.

We will wait upon the harvest moon
Let the rainstorm rumble on our heads
We will give these rising doubts to thunder
And still wait upon the harvest moon

Legon/Wheta, December 1975

Taflatse

I vowed I would not offend the ears of decent folk
But now, Sadzi, you've fed my thoughts with gall
My song will be the great whirlwind
that snatches your only decent cloth
sells your shame to inner thoughts of men
The devil's oath you swore
to defame my name
undo the fame I wove around my neck
with years of honest toil
O Sadzi, Sadzi Dzisavi, so
you would be the unforeseen landslide
that comes to dislodge the ancient rock
on which I sun my higher thoughts
You would undo my fame
But you Sadzi, you're yet to retrieve
the only underpants you ever wore in life
You pawned it years ago
for Paulie's pot of *tsukutsu*
And you want to undo my fame?
I Kodzo Kabada the evil
rope that binds, binding things that would not
be bound, binds the very things which
slip from hold of chains and copper wires
I'll bind your several shames
bind them tight with gentle
chords of my boundless song
sell your name in the market-place at noon

This dawn I met a young virgin in
tears, calling the clan to come witness her
woe. O Sadzi, Sadzi Dzisavi, to whose
dog did you give your
shame, you dare attempt a
rape in a public
lavatory?

God I hear never had the chance to polish you up
You ran away half-formed, haunting the world
playing the truant to eternity
Sadzi you're the evil
babe who pulled at the heartstrings of a sad
Mother. She died labouring to throw you out
And your father exchanged his manliness
for an eternity of shame
Today he walks the village lanes alone
eyes glued to his guilt quietly keeping
distance from all women: no other of
your kind
And ah Sadzi where is your sister now
who once upon a time strolled our lanes
with the easy poise of a natural queen
They say she fled at night to Hausaland
leaving behind a big burden of shame
and rumour says she's now
mother to your child
This monstrosity of yours Sadzi
Could this too be a gift of *Sé*?

Legon, 26 April 1976

Apologia: Prayer of the Damned

a pragmatist wakes in mid-dream
choked by echoes of apologies to sleep
Keepers of Hellgate spread out carpets for Heaven's
messengers
a bishop's cross swims in the palm-oil bowl
of a secret cult
trapped in vibrations of purified curses
of rebel deities

Cannot an oath be extracted from a lie?
Nor a sigh distilled from groans?
    standing barefoot on sun we watch
    our desires freeze into snow-flakes
    caught in the mixing-bowl of destinies
In absence of high priests who celebrates the mass for destooled
    deities?
        Give way this way . . .
        Heaven descends to consult with Hell
        over fate of Earth
god shall have to apologise to MAN

17 April 1975

The Passion-Gulf

Upon opposing banks
    we squat,
    our backs
            upon
            the smouldering wastelands of our heritage
mourning each other
    across
    the turbulence of flooded passions

What else could we do with
memories of boatfulls of hopes
caught mid-stream and set adrift on a river without a mouth?
        The agonies reflected in your tears
        respond to vibrations in my fears
        Your choice of despair
        hurts beyond repair
    in the dungeons of our sorrow

a volcano is grumbling . . .
it shall erupt . . .
Our cumulative anger shall burst
upon the strongholds of our torment
flooding our memory with heat-waves
fed by geysers in our heart
>> If the gulf cannot be bridged
>> It could be filled with corpses of our rage

17 April 1975

A Song for Silent Fears

for Doris at 22

This dirge, Doris, is the
smile
i owe your second
birth
It comes this late not for lack of tears
It takes so long to weave a song for silent fears

often so very often i've
watched your laughter grow timid
at echoes of secret doubts
heard your smile swoon away
from shadows of distant storms

Let this be
a lament
for final rites of wasted joys
a slow rhythm
for lingering burdens dragging their heart across

your twilight zone
Tomorrow tomorrow at midnight hour
you would glide with silences to blurred outskirts of life
you could beg our earth and carve a tomb for this corpse of a
    youth
Your right may hold the calabash of birthwaters
The left would grasp troubled spirit of home-made gin
With a new-found voice you would in confidence
pronounce the names
Old Deities, Ancestral Gods
Bestow your grace on a wayward child
with both your hands you'd turn the key
turning you back on still-born hopes of youth

O I know the burden of this song
carries the slow rhythm of a funereal dance
Let it also be
a chant an incantation
a ritual invocation of suspended joys
Let these receding echoes
go astray, transformed into excited booms
laid aside for coming festivals
The clouds you fear are now become
messengers of harvest joys, festive moods
riding low on shoulders of storms
The shadows in your eyes, they pause
watch watch how they quiver
in the new radiance of smiles
once gone blind with burnt-out rainbows
Put forth your hands, ah they tremble
they tremble to feel the pulse
urgent heart-beats of a soul
caught in final pangs of second birth
Come come close here
Under these silent eaves we
wait for happy screams of infant life

And while we wait
let us tell the soul to beware of doubts and frowns
O while we wait while we wait
do stretch forth your voice
catch the rhythm of this
dirge
this newly woven song this
smile
i owe your second
Birth

Legon, 9 November 1976

On Shores of Memory

for Akosua

Again and again and again
you may stand on shores of memory
watching the cold north winds
blasting the last day-dreams of youth

The longings in your heart fade into
nostalgic visions caught on crests
of waves rising jostling crumbling
into ripples and water-flakes

and if you stand if you stand too long
searching the skies for new planets
the sharpness of the winds may pierce
the smoothness of your gourd of tears
fears may spill into your soul
making slippery your last footsteps of life

see see how a million waves
dance upon the fury of the seas
ignoring the threats of rocks upon the shores
They abandon their burdens
to the motion of the currents
and loll in the last rhythms of life

In the spirit of the waves you see
the howlings in your soul fade into
echoes of the season's hallucinations
the blinding rays of this midday sun
dissolve into mirages where you catch
your feet breaking into a dance of grace
a festive dance into your twilight zone

Legon, 19 November 1976

Dance of the Hunchback

Mine is the dance of the hunchback
Along these quiet drains of town
I crawl my way with strain and shame
I leave paved streets to owners of the earth

He died. Mother's other only son. He died.
They said the doctor said
he died of innate poverty
Kinsmen came from distant quests
with precious things for parting gifts
pairs of velvet robes diamond rings
a glass coffin with rims of gold
cases of schnapps barrels of gun-powder
Each kind kinsman stood tall in our heart

an elder clears his ancient
throat, looks at me with loud
silence
I ignore the threat in his eye

Going down on knees
I whisper my brother's spirit-name
I whisper it thrice and offer all
I have: a tear and a song

At the wake-keeping this night
a cousin poet sells my shame in song
    a chief-mourner has laid a plot for a
    pauper's funeral
    kinsmen are not in it
    we weep this father
    whose line death snatches
    from an only proper son
    gives to a cripple to drag in dust

Public squares broad highways
and busy streets of town
I leave them all to owners of our earth
I crawl along quiet side-walks of life
With the hedge-hog and the crab
I carry a tedious destiny

    Mine is the dance of the hunchback
    In the valley behind my hill of shame
    I do my best to fall in step
    with rhythms of grace and pomp
    But the eyes of the world
    see only a moving bundle of fun
    and upon my chest they heap
    a growing burden of scorn

Wheta, 3 October 1976

The Last Dinner

I am the helpless fish
frying in your bowl of cooking oil
You lean against your kitchen wall
smiling with thoughts of coming feasts
But nature in time will call
You'll render accounts squatting on your heels
Your hunger returns with new demands
and I'll not be there to
feed the needs of
recurrent appetite

A Wreath of Tears

Sometimes
my mind fails
my heart dies within my thoughts

I caught my soul one noon
kneeling in desert sands
weaving a wreath of tears across the paths of moon

A seagull flew across my sky this dawn
killing me all over again
bringing back the day you went
away with wind with all our
dreams trailing behind your hopes written in
vapours across the sky

Today the skies are empty with waiting
waiting for wind to bring her next burden of clouds

Tomorrow
the rainmaker stands outside his sacred self
counts his steps across to life's outskirts
He stands from dawn till noon
searching for moon in light of day
At dusk he counts his steps backwards
through the village lanes
through the forest paths
back into the darkness of his sacred self
sowing the burden of our prayer in depths of his silence

Tonight
the virgins are gathered beneath our silk-cotton
They are selling dreams to moon
The joys they sing are eternal in their hearts
celebrating faith in death as
gateway to new desires of newer selves
I would reach out with my mind
for vibrations of their joy
but the void you left me in
still echoes in my soul
still
my mind fails
my heart dies within my thoughts

Legon, 15 January 1977

A Piece of Hope

I have searched the waves at dawn
for broken images of
the world we built upon the shores
with pools of troubled seas
The floods have gone to

where only storms may dwell
the beaches grown drowsy
sunning their naked breasts
amid murmurings of a million silences

I would rebuild our laughter
with echoes of the past
sleep at noon on remembered shores
dream of
doves perched on clouds across your milky-way
I would search the skies for new Edens
retrieve your voice from melodies of the spheres

The dolphins came riding the waves
a mermaid on their shoulders
She was casting your name upon the seas
whispering your laughter to the winds
They sat in the sand
purged my heart with a dirge, gave me
a piece of hope
           They will send you back some day

So now I search the waves at dawn
for broken images of
the world we built upon the shores
with pools of troubled seas
I would rebuild our laughter
with echoes of the past
dream at noon on forgotten shores
think of
souls asleep on moonbeams across my galaxy
I would search the skies for new Edens
reclaim your smile from rainbows in my soul

Wheta, 11 September 1976

Festival of Hopes

3rd Cock-crow
In the centre, where the midnight libation still lay in dregs,
a pointed peg broke through the soil, stood a foot above the
    Earth.
Upon
this peg, a needle perched.
Upon
that needle, a calabash came and sat.
Inside
this calabash, there was a void.
Then the Clan appeared.
Around the grounds they threw a ring,
their jaws still locked in a 7-day communion with Silence.
One by one,
Man by man
they stepped into the ring, bowed.
Publicly, silently, they shed their private fears
draining their secret cares
into that big brown calabash, container of the Clan's tears.

Noon
A step away from the calabash of public fears
Earth cracked and produced a neck without a head;
the neck rose and revealed a body slightly pregnant;
the body produced no legs: on a flat bottom it sat:
a gourd.
Inside
that gourd, there was a void.
Again the Clan came
Around the gourd, they wove a ring,
their teeth still clenched in a cruel gruelling duel with Life.
Two by two
Man and wife

Widow with orphan
they hopped into the ring, bowed.
Quietly, openly, they poured out their secret toils,
draining their private sweat
into the deep brown gourd pregnant with the Clan's broils.

Dusk
3 steps from the calabash of tears and gourd of toils
the Earth pushed up a hearth.
Into
this hearth, dried wood piled up.
Upon
that pile, a pot installed herself
Inside
this iron pot, there was a void.
Screaming and shrieking and groaning and moaning,
armed with muscle bone and nerve,
eyes swimming in flooded passions of souls possessed,
the Clan rushed, charged, stopped.
In the gathering dusk of that festive eve,
each clansman gnashed his teeth
                    and bit his lips
                        and vomited blood
                            into
                                the void which filled that pot.
Upon no signal, the chant began – low, heavy, nostalgic:
a terrible valediction offered in memoriam to a suspended
    millennium
Echoes, they say, fly fast to closed chapters of life,
stirring frozen heartbeats of older worlds.
The chants rose deep, mingling with
re-awakened rhythms of *atrikpui* and *adzogbo*,
bringing vigorous memories of
                        mortalised heroes
                        and
                        ethnic vendettas.

The rhythms boiled to a frenzy, driving
Clansmen crazy with re-juvenated glories of
                                younger worlds.

A clap of clouds, a shaft of light
and a distraught meteor struck the pile of wood,
inflaming the hearth, the flames engulfing the pot of blood,
flooding the festive grounds with a glory
made hoary by crazed shadows of dazed clansmen
each wrestling with his mortal self in
a jubilant desperation to evoke the second self.
The flames made a triple leap and grabbed
the gourd of sweat and calabash of tears.
Excitement seized an old clansman – he tossed
himself above the flames and landed neat
                                in the pot of boiling blood.
He died chanting an ancient song of Life
The Clan forgot the chorus.
But they jumped and danced,
embracing and shaking hands,
                    watching the flames
                    dwindling into
                    a pencil
                    of smoke
                    which
                    shot
                    in-
                    to
                    higher realms, laden with
                    evaporated impurities for symbolic
                    purification in distilleries of Destiny.

27 January–11 April 1975

90